PROMISES FOR A FRUITFUL LIFE

✦   ✦   ✦

Visit Tyndale online at tyndale.com.

Visit Tyndale Momentum online at tyndalemomentum.com.

Visit Beth Moore online at lproof.org.

TYNDALE, Tyndale's quill logo, *Tyndale Momentum*, and the Tyndale Momentum logo are registered trademarks of Tyndale House Publishers. Tyndale Momentum is the nonfiction imprint of Tyndale House Publishers, Carol Stream, Illinois.

Promises for a Fruitful Life

Designed by Dean H. Renninger

Lettering by Lindsey Bergsma

Published in association with Yates & Yates (www.yates2.com).

For information about special discounts for bulk purchases, please contact Tyndale House Publishers at csresponse@tyndale.com, or call 1-800-323-9400.

Names: Moore, Beth, author.
Title: Promises for a fruitful life / Beth Moore.
Description: Carol Stream, Illinois : Tyndale House Publishers, 2020.
Identifiers: LCCN 2019041686 (print) | LCCN 2019041687 (ebook) | ISBN
   9781496440921 (trade paperback) | ISBN 9781496440938 (kindle edition) |
   ISBN 9781496440945 (epub) | ISBN 9781496440952 (epub)
Subjects: LCSH: God—Promises—Meditations.
Classification: LCC BT180.P7 M66 2020 (print) | LCC BT180.P7 (ebook) |
   DDC 242—dc23
LC record available at https://lccn.loc.gov/2019041686
LC ebook record available at https://lccn.loc.gov/2019041687

Printed in the United States of America

26	25	24	23	22	21	20
8	7	6	5	4	3	2

BETH MOORE

+ + +

PROMISES FOR A
fruitful life

TYNDALE
MOMENTUM®

The Tyndale nonfiction imprint

When you produce much fruit, you are my
true disciples. This brings great glory to my
Father. . . . You didn't choose me. I chose you.
I appointed you to go and produce lasting
fruit, so that the Father will give you whatever
you ask for, using my name.

JOHN 15:8, 16

INTRODUCTION

We were created to contribute, fashioned to bring who we are and what we have to the human mix to add some measure of benefit. This was true even in Eden's unmarred paradise. God said to Adam and Eve, in so many words, *Add to it! Work the ground! And the two of you, be fruitful and multiply. Fill the earth!*

Jesus elevated the concept to another stratosphere by taking individuals He'd given abundant life to and, by the power of His own Spirit, making their contributions matter not just temporally, as He did with Adam and Eve, but eternally.

God means for us to be profoundly effective. That longing in us to contribute, to do

1

something worthwhile, isn't just a self-consumed dream. If we follow Jesus, that's what we can hope to expect from life.

And being fruitful isn't some stale and banal duty. It directly affects how happy we are, because engaging in what God is doing is the only thing that gives us true satisfaction and peace.

God wants you to flourish in Him. Every last thing He plants in your life is intended for that purpose. If we give ourselves fully to His faithful ways, mysterious and painful though they may be at times, we will find that it's all part of the process that enables us to grow and bear fruit.

The Bible is full of God's promises for us. In this book, I've captured some of my favorite promises about the abundance Jesus has in mind for us. Please join me as we walk through thirty-one precious promises from God's Word.

Beth Moore

WHEN YOU FEEL AS THOUGH YOUR LIFE LACKS PURPOSE . . .

✦   ✦   ✦

The LORD will work out his plans for my life—
*   for your faithful love, O LORD, endures*
*   forever.*
*   Don't abandon me, for you made me.*
PSALM 138:8

In life, so many unexplainable things happen that can make a person feel like everything is one enormous accident. Some dots never do seem to connect. Your present job may appear to have nothing to do with your last job. You may feel like what you were trained to do has no link to what you're actually doing.

We long for continuity, for some semblance of purpose—anything that might suggest we're on the right track. Instead, we feel like ashes, leftovers from a bygone fire, blown aimlessly by the wind. We feel like we're not even important enough to be forgotten, because we were never known in the first place.

Our perceptions can be very convincing, but God tells us the truth. Nothing about our existence is accidental. We were known before we knew we were alive. We were planned and, as a matter of fact, planted on this earth for this moment in time.

WHEN YOU GROW IMPATIENT WAITING FOR YOUR LIFE TO CHANGE . . .

+ + +

This vision is for a future time.
  It describes the end, and it will be fulfilled.
If it seems slow in coming, wait patiently,
  for it will surely take place.
  It will not be delayed.

HABAKKUK 2:3

Have you ever wondered why God goes to the trouble of sanctifying us? He could instantly zap us into His image the moment we decide to follow Jesus, or He could transport us into heaven at the moment of our conversion.

Why would He opt for taking us through the long, drawn-out process of planting, watering, pruning, and harvesting? Why would he choose to slowly grow what He could have simply created already grown? Why on earth would He go to the trouble to plant a garden forced to sprout rather than commanding it into existence, full bloom? Why leave His desk and get His pant legs soiled?

Because God likes watching things grow.

He rolls up His sleeves, puts palms to the dirt, and begins putting the pieces of our lives together in a way that matters.

WHEN YOU FEEL LIKE YOU DON'T FIT IN . . .

✦ ✦ ✦

You are altogether beautiful, my darling,
beautiful in every way.

SONG OF SONGS 4:7

Over the years, I've had the hardest time figuring out where I belong. I'll think, *This is it!* and the next thing I know, that hostile dog of insecurity starts nipping at my heels again, telling me I'm out of place.

Do you ever get that same feeling? After countless conversations, I've come to the conclusion that what most of us have in common is the feeling that we're misfits.

Maybe nothing is more normal than feeling a bit abnormal. Maybe feeling comfortable in our own skin means coming to the realization that we weren't created to feel particularly comfortable in this skin.

But God didn't choose you because nobody better was within arm's reach. God's arm is neither short nor weak (Isaiah 59:1). If He chose you, He did so on purpose. Ephesians 1:4 declares with spectacular clarity, "Even before he made the world, God loved us and chose us in Christ."

If you've been chosen by God, there is no room for equivocation: you matter.

WHEN YOU FEEL
UNSETTLED . . .

+ + +

You will show me the way of life,
granting me the joy of your presence
and the pleasures of living with you forever.

PSALM 16:11

Nothing can get more confusing than feeling planted somewhere you're sure is home only to be uprooted and transplanted somewhere else. Without warning, you face the prospect of having to start all over again. Your future seemed clear. Your people were near. And now you feel like a stranger in a foreign land.

Sometimes you'll stay in that unfamiliar land for longer than you ever imagined. Other times God will pluck you up and move you right back to your homeland, only for you to come to the bewildering realization that although the place hasn't changed, you have.

Nothing haunts us more than our search for a sense of place. As it turns out, true belonging is found only in the sovereign palm of God. There alone we find our place, even amid the seasons of moving, planting, uprooting, and replanting.

WHEN YOU
NEED REST . . .

+ + +

*Jesus said, "Come to me, all of you who are
weary and carry heavy burdens, and I will give
you rest. Take my yoke upon you. Let me teach
you, because I am humble and gentle at heart,
and you will find rest for your souls. For my
yoke is easy to bear, and the burden
I give you is light."*
MATTHEW 11:28-30

We live our lives looking for home. But it's only when we find our place in Him that we find rest.

David said it with beautiful simplicity: "I am at rest in God alone" (Psalm 62:1, CSB). Though the path to this discovery is often painful, the discovery itself can be a relief—and not only to us. It gives us space to spread out and grow, and it relieves our other loves of a burden too big to carry.

And there we can bear mysterious fruit.

WHEN YOU FEEL
INSIGNIFICANT . . .

✦   ✦   ✦

Don't be afraid, little flock. For it gives your
Father great happiness to give you the Kingdom.
LUKE 12:32

Maybe you feel passed over. Invisible. Unviable. Maybe you believe that God calls other people to contribute and use their gifts for His noble purposes, but your own branch seems bare. Perhaps the last thing you feel like is the answer to a promise. Or perhaps the way it looks to you, at one time you showed great promise and your gifts were affirmed, but for some baffling reason, all that promise seemed to fizzle out and amount to nothing.

If that's you, then I want you to know that if you are in Christ, your life is attached to the very One who is life. Nothing about you means nothing, because He who defines you and makes use of you is everything. Your identity is in the One whose name reverberates above every other name and whose fame endures forever.

Your fruit will outlast your life. You can't always see the effects, because they are eternal, but one day you will. One day you will see that you couldn't have been more significant if you'd tried.

WHEN YOU FEEL
LIKE YOU DON'T
MEASURE UP . . .

+   +   +

Seek the Kingdom of God above all else,
and live righteously, and he will give you
everything you need.

MATTHEW 6:33

By God's design, these mortal bodies are fraught with limits and bound by certain natural laws. If we don't eat, we starve. If we don't sleep, we die. If we don't ever stop, we drop. If we abandon what we're doing to answer every text, we'll never finish any significant task. None of us is the exception. None of us can do a thousand things to the glory of God, but we can do several.

When you're on your deathbed, which ones will you want to have chosen? Have guts enough to choose the things that matter now.

WHEN YOU FEEL REJECTED OR UNLOVED . . .

+   +   +

We know, dear brothers and sisters,
that God loves you and has chosen you
to be his own people.

1 THESSALONIANS 1:4

There is no song like a song of unrequited love. Everyone knows one. Most everyone has one. It can play anywhere—at a party, in a restaurant, in a salon, over the sound system in a store—and suddenly you're right back in that moment. Feeling sick inside. Jolted. Perhaps you fish the song back out on purpose because something has you remembering. You replay it because you wonder now, after all this time, if it was real.

It was. You know by how long it takes you to shake out of the replay after the music stops. We have nothing more intimate to offer another living soul than our love. Authentic affection cannot exist apart from vulnerability. A heart that is wide open to love is wide open to hurt. We could seal off our hearts in an attempt to avoid being hurt, but in doing so, we'd also shut ourselves off from relationships that make life matter.

WHEN YOU FEEL LIKE YOU'RE GETTING TOO CAUGHT UP IN THE WORLD . . .

✦ ✦ ✦

Don't copy the behavior and customs of this world, but let God transform you into a new person by changing the way you think. Then you will learn to know God's will for you, which is good and pleasing and perfect.

ROMANS 12:2

Only one thing is worse than producing no fruit: producing bad fruit. Since the Father calls Jesus-followers to live immensely fruitful lives, it stands to reason that no question is more relevant than this: What kind of fruit are we producing? We can't see fruit the way God can, but with His help, we are fully capable of distinguishing between good fruit and bad fruit.

What's the best way to tell what kind of fruit is being produced in your life? Look for evidence of the fruit of the Spirit—things like "love, joy, peace, patience, kindness, goodness, faithfulness, gentleness, and self-control" (Galatians 5:22-23). If the action or approach is quenching qualities of the Spirit, it's producing bad fruit. If it's evidencing qualities of the Spirit, it's producing good fruit.

WHEN YOU FEEL LIKE YOU'RE RUNNING ON EMPTY . . .

✦   ✦   ✦

The LORD replied, "I will personally go with you, Moses, and I will give you rest—everything will be fine for you."

EXODUS 33:14

None of us can do everything. None of us can please everyone. None of us has access to more than twenty-four hours a day or to more than seven days a week. We have to resist the temptation to promote more than we actually perform.

If we think we have a God who only convicts and never encourages, who only tells us what's wrong with us and never what's right, we've probably created a god made in the image of a human authority who scarred us.

The truth is, we are safe and loved by God—no matter what kind of fruit we're currently producing.

WHEN YOUR DAILY
STRUGGLES FEEL
OVERWHELMING . . .

+ + +

*Dear brothers and sisters, when troubles of any
kind come your way, consider it an opportunity
for great joy. For you know that when your faith
is tested, your endurance has a chance to grow.
So let it grow, for when your endurance is fully
developed, you will be perfect and complete,
needing nothing.*

JAMES 1:2-4

I don't know what your climb is like right now. Maybe your muscles are burning from the fatigue of a hard marriage or an arduous job or the scaling of a painful relationship. It seems like you've been hiking for half a lifetime already, and the worst part is that you can't even see the top.

There may be days when you grow weary of climbing and you long for flatter terrain. But the slopes are overlaid with tremendous purpose. Your struggles will not be wasted, even if it feels that way now. God uses them to tilt us toward the light, to drain the sludge from our hearts with spring rains, and to offer us a view of the landscape that will one day turn into vision.

The rocky soil in the life of the Jesus-follower is not so much about failure as it is about fruitfulness. One of these days, after we've seen Christ face-to-face, He may get around to saying something like, "Remember all those hard things I grew you through? I did you a favor. You can thank Me now." And I bet we will, and on that side of things, I bet we'll mean it.

WHEN YOU FEEL UNWORTHY OF JESUS' LOVE . . .

✦ ✦ ✦

When you obey my commandments, you remain in my love, just as I obey my Father's commandments and remain in his love.

JOHN 15:10

Somewhere deep inside, I think many of us believe Jesus spends time in our company primarily out of obligation, as if we're an annoying, misfit appendage He's stuck with. After all, He promised to be with us always. He has to be true to His word.

It's easy to get it in our heads that we're tolerated more than enjoyed. My guess is that most of us wouldn't picture him eagerly desiring to spend time with us, yet that's precisely what Scripture says of His final evening before death. What He wanted most of all was to share a meal with His followers.

Jesus wants to shift your securities so that you will abide in Him alone, not in other people, places, and things. He knows that those things are bereft of the power to anchor, oxygenate, and animate you the way His Spirit does.

If you're in Christ, He is your true Vine, whether you realize it or not. But a whole new way of flourishing begins when you know it. When you count on it. When you live like it.

WHEN YOU'RE STRUGGLING TO WAIT ON THE LORD . . .

+   +   +

I say to myself, "The LORD is my inheritance;
    therefore, I will hope in him!"
The LORD is good to those who depend on him,
    to those who search for him.
So it is good to wait quietly
    for salvation from the LORD.

LAMENTATIONS 3:24-26

In one sense, abiding sounds like the easiest command for a Jesus-follower to undertake. It means resting in the One who is stronger than we are, wiser than we are, and more powerful than we are—and who loves us and defends us.

But for most of us, the not-doing is infinitely more difficult than the doing. Give us a to-do list or a deadline or an assignment, but for the love, please don't ask us to let go and be still.

You need not worry that all this abiding will get boring. There's no getting used to Jesus. One of the best parts of abiding in Christ is staying close enough to catch a glimpse of what He decides to reveal.

WHEN YOU FEEL
COMPELLED TO
GO IT ALONE . . .

✦　✦　✦

*I am the vine; you are the branches. Those who
remain in me, and I in them, will produce much
fruit. For apart from me you can do nothing.*
JOHN 15:5

We prefer to do things ourselves, in our own way. But could it be that what God loves most about His relationship with us is precisely what we do not love about it? He loves to be with us, sit with us, and walk with us. He didn't need disciples. He could have accomplished every task He desired without them. He chose the disciples to have "part with Him" (John 13:8, CSB), to partner with Him (2 Corinthians 6:1).

God doesn't need us, either. He could accomplish all He wills from the throne of heaven. He wants us with Him. He longs for a relationship with us. While God desires the relational, however, we humans tend toward the transactional.

We say to the Alpha and Omega, "Give me the plan from A to Z, and leave it to me." We forget that He came to be Immanuel, God with us.

We're all capable of doing good work. Abiding in Christ is about doing what we can't do on our own and becoming who we can't be on our own.

WHEN YOU'RE NOT SURE WHERE GOD IS LEADING YOU . . .

✛ ✛ ✛

This is my command—be strong and courageous! Do not be afraid or discouraged. For the LORD your God is with you wherever you go.

JOSHUA 1:9

During so much of this walk with God, we feel blindfolded. Certain seasons are pocked with such random events that we decide all is helter-skelter. Other seasons seem so illustriously orchestrated that the ties between events are like streamers of spun gold. From the very beginning, God geared the faith walk to be relational, not informational. The latter was always intended for the sake of the former.

Walking transpires step by step. It demands patience. Pacing. God's directional leading for our personal lives often unfurls in bits of light between shadows. He says His word is a lamp to our feet, which offers us the assurance of arm's length direction when He says, "Go."

WHEN YOU FEEL ALONE ON YOUR JOURNEY . . .

+   +   +

*Teach these new disciples to obey all the
commands I have given you. And be sure of this:
I am with you always, even to the end
of the age.*

MATTHEW 28:20

Following Jesus isn't just about a prescribed set of rules or a certain set of behaviors. It's about being tethered to Jesus like He's oxygen—it's about being in His presence at every moment. When you're with someone you love, it doesn't matter what you're doing; it's about doing it together.

Being a branch to the true Vine means living with Christ, breathing with Christ, doing day-to-day life with Christ. It's the ongoing awareness of His presence, even when there's no feeling of His presence. Our lives become witness to His with-ness.

Jesus is our staying power in all our going. If you'll stay while you go, you may not always know where you're going. But you can know that wherever you end up, He will walk you there.

WHEN THE NEEDS
OF OTHERS WEIGH
YOU DOWN . . .

+ + +

*Most important of all, continue to show deep
love for each other, for love covers a multitude
of sins. Cheerfully share your home with those
who need a meal or a place to stay. God has
given each of you a gift from his great variety
of spiritual gifts. Use them well to serve
one another.*

1 PETER 4:8-10

Part of abiding with Christ means abiding with other people too. We are here to help people in Jesus' name. This seems elementary, as if it should go without saying, but somehow I have to say it to myself continually.

When we feel like people are finally about to drive us entirely over the edge, we are in precisely the right shape for a deep breath and a momentary break. Then it's time to bear in mind once again that people are the point.

They need our tenderness. They need our flexibility. They may just need us to sit with them, to abide with them.

WHEN YOU
FALL SHORT
OF YOUR GOALS . . .

+ + +

Let's not get tired of doing what is good.
At just the right time we will reap a harvest
of blessing if we don't give up.

GALATIANS 6:9

We've all been there—on the cusp of something fresh and wonderful, only to have our starry-eyed love dampened, our awakened passion quenched, our budding victory vanquished. This kind of trimming feels unjust—cruel, even.

You can see the budding. It's right there before your eyes. You can taste the breakthrough on the tip of your tongue. But just before it comes to fruition—faith made sight—your breakthrough ends up looking suspiciously more like a breakdown.

What you must trust in these moments is that anything God breaks down is intended to build you up. Anything He cuts off is to give breathing space to what He's adding on.

It may take a while for joy to come in the midst of pruning, but it is inevitable. Fruitfulness is always finally felicity.

WHEN YOU'RE STRUGGLING WITH PAIN AND LOSS . . .

+   +   +

We know that God causes everything to work
together for the good of those who love God and
are called according to his purpose for them.
ROMANS 8:28

Sometimes growing can look a lot like shrinking. You may not have the faintest clue that God is busily making you more productive, because what seems far clearer is that He is intent on killing you. In gardening, the term for this is *pruning*—cutting back old growth to generate new.

For some of us, pruning begins early in life; others may remain relatively intact until the later decades of life. By no means is all loss pruning, but pruning can certainly look like loss. It can also look like relational fracture or like failure, weakness, or sickness, because it involves paring back in some capacity.

But God uses it all. If we allow His shears to do their work, the purpose is always the same: growth.

WHEN YOU ARE
FACING OBSTACLES ...

+   +   +

Don't be afraid, for I am with you.
   Don't be discouraged, for I am your God.
I will strengthen you and help you.
   I will hold you up with my victorious
     right hand.

ISAIAH 41:10

God never calls us to something only to abandon us once we've arrived. He's at work whether or not we see a whit of evidence.

The truth is, you were indeed called, and your calling is irrevocable. Whatever challenges or setbacks you encounter are for the sake of your calling, not in spite of it.

Difficulty is paramount to producing. Without it, you won't be able to faithfully steward your gifting.

WHEN GOD
FEELS DISTANT
OR ABSENT . . .

✢   ✢   ✢

*Be strong and courageous! Do not be afraid
and do not panic before them. For the LORD
your God will personally go ahead of you.
He will neither fail you nor abandon you.*

DEUTERONOMY 31:6

At times God is too close for us to see. We lose sight of how He's working until months or years later, when we're able to step back and gain a broader perspective.

At times we're in the dark because God is revealing some aspect of His glory that's more than we can stare straight in the face.

The beauty in the darkness is that God is close enough to cover us with His hand. Often at the end of a tremendously intense season, He'll grace us with a glimpse of His back. He gives us just enough evidence of His presence for us to realize He was there all along—not as a spectator or even just as a protector, but as Lord over all.

WHEN YOU'RE DEALING WITH PAIN AND SUFFERING . . .

+ + +

The LORD is close to the brokenhearted;
*   he rescues those whose spirits are crushed.*

PSALM 34:18

God is never closer to us than He is during the pruning process. He can't avoid holding a branch when He's pinching off blooms with His thumbnail. With God as Gardener, pruning is always a hands-on endeavor. He can't let us go when He's cutting us back. His tending is never impersonal. Never mechanical.

What most of us didn't expect when we took up with Him was that His presence would sometimes cause pain. We expected His presence to relieve pain and, to our great relief, it usually does. God cuts back a fruitful vine only to increase its fruitfulness.

WHEN LIFE'S PROBLEMS FEEL OVERWHELMING . . .

+ + +

I have told you all this so that you may have peace in me. Here on earth you will have many trials and sorrows. But take heart, because I have overcome the world.

JOHN 16:33

God doesn't promise that we'll avoid pain because we follow Him. He doesn't promise that we'll escape trauma or abuse or divorce or illness or death. But He does promise a way up. A way through. Or a way out.

If we offer what we've experienced to Him, in all its horror and ugliness, and receive His offer to redeem all that occurred, He will bring fruit from it.

WHEN YOU ARE STRUGGLING TO FIND MEANING IN LOSS . . .

✦   ✦   ✦

I am convinced that nothing can ever separate
us from God's love. Neither death nor life,
neither angels nor demons, neither our fears for
today nor our worries about tomorrow—not
even the powers of hell can separate us from
God's love. No power in the sky above or in the
earth below—indeed, nothing in all creation will
ever be able to separate us from the love of God
that is revealed in Christ Jesus our Lord.
ROMANS 8:38-39

Unless you're among the rarest exceptions, something terrible has happened to you at one point or another. The death of a dream. The death of a friendship. And sometimes worst of all, the physical death of someone you love.

Here's the big reveal: it didn't kill you. The remaining question is whether you're willing to expose yourself to the odd concoction of life and death that makes you grow.

What use are we here on this earth without a whit of death in our lives? What depth do we have? What proof of our faith? What evidence of perseverance?

What do we have to say to people in need, in pain, in doubt, in despair? How can we help those who feel nothing but dead if we've known nothing of death ourselves? What glimpse do we have to offer of a Savior whose death gave us life?

On those days when it seems like God is silent, know that He is using even the most painful and seemingly hopeless experiences to help you grow.

WHEN YOU'RE GOING THROUGH A DIFFICULT SEASON . . .

+   +   +

*"I know the plans I have for you," says the
LORD. "They are plans for good and not for
disaster, to give you a future and a hope."*
JEREMIAH 29:11

When we're going through a difficult season, wouldn't the best news of all be that life would simply go back to normal someday? When the framework of our daily existence gets completely dismantled and the landscape around us grows increasingly unrecognizable, our strongest longing is seldom prosperity. What we yearn for is normalcy.

We don't tend to ask for the moon when we've lost all we've known. We just want some semblance of our old lives back.

The hard truth is, there's no real going back. But once we get up again, there can be a going forward. In His faithfulness, God sees to it what we thought was the end isn't the end after all.

WHEN YOU FEEL AS THOUGH YOU HAVE LOST EVERYTHING . . .

+ + +

Forget all that—
it is nothing compared to what I am going
to do.
For I am about to do something new.
See, I have already begun! Do you not see it?
I will make a pathway through the wilderness.
I will create rivers in the dry wasteland.

ISAIAH 43:18-19

Invariably in life, unwanted changes occur. Crises happen. Catastrophes invade our days without warning. The pleasant field that once surrounded us has been scorched and razed. Whether or not our physical surroundings ever again resemble what we once knew, we can bear fruit again!

Maybe right now that promise doesn't mean a lot. You don't want to grow something new. You want to return to your old life. You want everything to look exactly like it once did.

I understand. But in time, finding fruitfulness again will make more difference than you can imagine. If we can't have our treasured yesterday back, at least tomorrow can matter.

The wonder of fruit bearing is that something meaningful can come from even the meanest of seasons.

WHEN IT'S TEMPTING TO HIDE FROM LIFE'S PROBLEMS . . .

✦   ✦   ✦

You, too, must be patient. Take courage,
for the coming of the Lord is near.
JAMES 5:8

When we're outside, exposed to the elements, we're reminded how little we really do control. We're hit afresh with the revelation that we're not as self-reliant as we thought we were. It's not that we can handle our challenges indoors; it's that it's easier to believe our illusions of control.

The fact is, real beauty is found out there under the same sky as vulnerability. I'm not suggesting we can't die out there—we can. But we will most certainly die if we stay inside forever.

Given enough time in the artificial light, within our insulated walls, our fruit will dry up and our branches will wither. Tap water simply can't compare with the feeling of rain on our faces. Hearing the wind is a paltry substitute for feeling it whip through our hair.

Shut yourself in from the pain of exposure, and you'll also miss the sunset, where orange turns to purple and restores our souls.

When we over-insulate ourselves, we're protecting ourselves right out of our callings.

WHEN BAD THINGS JUST KEEP HAPPENING . . .

+ + +

Be truly glad. There is wonderful joy ahead, even though you must endure many trials for a little while. These trials will show that your faith is genuine. It is being tested as fire tests and purifies gold—though your faith is far more precious than mere gold. So when your faith remains strong through many trials, it will bring you much praise and glory and honor on the day when Jesus Christ is revealed to the whole world.

I PETER I:6-7

Nobody told me a remotely productive life would involve quite so much manure. That's why I'm telling you. If you want to live an immensely fruitful life, you will have to deal with substantial piles of it. I wish I could tell you otherwise, but we both know better.

There are plenty of people willing to provide the manure for you. You don't have to go out looking for it; it will find you. You'll go through an ordeal or an attack, an assessment or a critique that even years later you will think had no constructive element whatsoever. It just seems meaningless.

But it's not! God can use it as potent fertilizer to bring about some fine fruit in your life!

WHEN THE HITS JUST KEEP ON COMING . . .

✦   ✦   ✦

The temptations in your life are no different from what others experience. And God is faithful. He will not allow the temptation to be more than you can stand. When you are tempted, he will show you a way out so that you can endure.

1 CORINTHIANS 10:13

You might be tempted to think that God tricked you into something and then refused to support you. Or that He talked you into something beyond your natural abilities and then abandoned you, leaving you to fend for yourself.

What you're going through is how it goes for nearly everyone who's serious about serving Jesus. If this is the season you find yourself in, I can fairly confidently assure you it won't always be this brutal. It will always be hard. At times it will be horrific. But this season of eye-bulging, nobody-ever-said-it-would-be-like-this pestilence won't last forever.

If you're in a season of pestilence, fight it out. If you've gotten sloppy, tighten it up. If you're neck deep in sin, repent. Go back on your face before God. Open a Bible and plant your nose in it. Memorize Scripture. Learn how to fast and pray. Quit talking *about* Jesus more than you talk *to* Him.

You'll come out on the other side of every well-fought fight knowing Jesus in a way you formerly believed He couldn't be known.

WHEN IT'S TIME TO SHARE YOUR FRUIT . . .

*Let your good deeds shine out for all to see, so
that everyone will praise your heavenly Father.*
MATTHEW 5:16

Love God. Love people. That's what we're here to do. "The fruit of the Spirit is love" (Galatians 5:22, esv). Without love, all fruit is plastic. The fruit of our lives, in all its forms and manifold graces, is truest to the Vine when it's generously extended and accessible to strangers and aliens of any kind.

We know that we, too, were once wanderers. We, too, were once slaves. We, too, were once poor in spirit. But now, in Christ, we have found a home. We have been set free. We have been made rich!

WHEN YOU'RE WONDERING IF ALL OF THE PAIN, SUFFERING, AND FRUSTRATION IS WORTH IT . . .

+   +   +

All of God's promises have been fulfilled in Christ with a resounding "Yes!" And through Christ, our "Amen" (which means "Yes") ascends to God for his glory.

2 CORINTHIANS 1:20

I think God gives us occasional inklings of how happy we'll be when we're united with Him. We experience punctures in this bubble of temporal madness—times when eternal bliss seems to bleed through.

We know a better world is coming, though we don't know when and though even the best theologians can't explain exactly how. We know an eternal God won't stop until He has brought everything full circle. We know because He said so. As surely as God redeemed humans from the curse of sin through the Cross, He will redeem the earth from the curse of sin that caused the ground to rebel against the work of human hands!

One thing is for certain, whatever we have coming, it will be the best possible everything!